D0582112

CHICKEN SOUP FOR THE SOUL®
CELEBRATES MOTHERS

CHICKEN SOUP FOR THE SOUL® CELEBRATES MOTHERS

A Collection in Words and Photographs by

Jack Canfield & Mark Victor Hansen

and

Sharon J. Wohlmuth

Health Communications, Inc.
Deerfield Beach, Florida

www.hcibooks.com
www.chickensoupforthesoul.com

Subject matter, locality and/or people in the photographs may not be the actual locality or people in the stories. Names of certain individuals have been changed to protect their identity.

Library of Congress Cataloging-in-Publication Data
is available from the Library of Congress

ISBN 0-7573-0103-7

Publisher: Health Communications, Inc.
3201 S.W. 15th Street
Deerfield Beach, FL 33442-8190

Cover design by Larissa Hise Henoch
Inside book design by Lawna Patterson Oldfield

CONTENTS

THE DAY IT ALL CAME TOGETHER

March can be cold in Texas. I hadn't expected that. A transplanted Yankee, by way of a slight if forgivable detour through Virginia, I viewed Texas with the same avidity I did a pit viper. In my imagination, Texas was a land of endless deserts. Rattlesnakes curled up on the porch, and armadillos wandered the streets. My move to San Antonio, courtesy of the Air Force to which I owed my time if not my soul, might as well have been a one-way shot to the moon.

It was in that alien landscape of cacti, fire ants, scorpions, armadillos, rattlesnakes, and a purposeful, somewhat lunatic roadrunner that traversed our cul-de-sac every afternoon at three without fail, that I became pregnant with our first child.

We hadn't exactly been trying, but we hadn't exactly been careful either. We had sidled up to parenthood gradually, practicing first on three cats and a golden retriever. The baby was conceived during a playoff game between the Washington Redskins and the Chicago Bears, somewhere in the third quarter, around the twentieth yard line of the Bears. The Redskins went on to win the Super Bowl that year, a prelude of things to come, and after our initial astonished exchange ("Are you sure?" "Of course, I'm sure. Look, the stick is blue!"), we accepted that the pregnancy just *was,* like morning coffee or taxes.

But I was not excited. I was a professional. I had a career. Ergo, pregnancy was a temporary way station on the road to something called motherhood, a hazy concept blurred at the margins by images of June and Ward, and Archie and Edith. After a wretched first trimester, when one sympathetic obstetrician observed that if men had to endure the raging hormonal imbalances pregnant women did, they would end up gasping on the floor like beached fish, I had adopted a somewhat detached attitude. There was nothing I could do about the alien invader whose presence reshaped my body before my eyes. She—for I knew "it" was a "she" by the sixteenth week—was a nameless entity that squiggled and kicked and rolled and had a knack for getting up when I most wanted to sleep.

Predictably, my parents were thrilled. My in-laws gushed. I received countless, indulgent smiles as I waddled back and forth, though men stopped whistling. (That was discouraging. Of course, wandering around in an Air Force maternity uniform wasn't helpful. The uniform was like a light blue parachute: a pull of the ripcord at the start of each month, and a new panel billowed out.) Total strangers approached me in the supermarket and patted my belly, as if I was their private Buddha. Yet despite my pediatrician-husband's assurances that I would soon "glow," I wasn't in the least bit incandescent. I didn't place my hands protectively across my abdomen the way women did in the movies. I didn't coo, and I didn't knit booties. There was one bad moment, in my fourth month, when I had an almost irresistible urge to buy a sewing machine. I paced the floor in front of a row of Singers and gnawed my nails. I think I finally wandered over to the living room section of the store, found a sleeper sofa on sale, and lay down, waiting for that feeling to go away. It did.

I remember, too, that my mother assured me that the anonymous lump in my stomach would develop her own little personality. I was not convinced, and to prove who was in charge here, I resisted picking a name.

One thing I did religiously was exercise. No puffy ankles for me, no hundred-pound weight gain. I swam incessantly. The one thing I did enjoy about Texas, besides breakfast fajitas, was the fact that I could swim outdoors year-round. There was a pool on the training side of the base, and I would swim a mile every day, without fail. As with naming the baby, I refused to buy a maternity suit and give in to what my aunt euphemistically called "my condition." My black Speedo stretched very nicely, thanks, and I think after his initial double take, the lifeguard got used to seeing the equivalent of a big, black water beetle.

Most of all, I wanted to prove that pregnancy was no obstacle. So one cold March afternoon—cold being a relative term in Texas—I pulled up to the pool, lugged my stuff into the locker room, and stuffed myself into my suit.

There was no one else insane enough to be at the pool except the lifeguard who had trudged out to his seat and huddled, miserable in a gray sweatshirt and beach towel. I wandered up to the edge of the pool and dipped my toe in. The water was like ice. I pulled my toe out. I caught the lifeguard looking hopeful.

Wrong-o, I thought. *Just watch me.*

I crossed to the steps, and gingerly let myself down into the water. The water wasn't just *like* ice; it *was* ice. Any sane person would have leapt from the water, called it a day and had a mug of hot chocolate.

Not me. Gritting my teeth, I persevered, and it was when the water hit the bottom of my belly that the baby reacted. Suddenly, my belly levitated. I was stunned. To be absolutely sure, I backed up the steps. The water receded, and my belly sagged. I counted to ten then got in again up to mid-abdomen. Now my belly didn't just rise; it lurched, and there was an odd, scrambling movement. It was as if the baby was trying to climb into my throat—anywhere it was warm. Then she kicked me, hard.

An image flashed in my mind: my baby yanking on her umbilical cord and yelping, "What the heck are you doing up there?"

I couldn't help it. I started to laugh. I'm sure the lifeguard thought I'd lost my mind. But in that instant, the baby went from being an anonymous alien fluttering around in my belly to assuming her own uniqueness, and she wanted to be very sure I understood that she was not amused.

So I didn't swim that day, or any other day in March of that year. And that night, my husband held me at arm's length and studied me with care.

"What?" I asked.

He folded me into his arms. "You glow."

We had chili that night, with lots of jalapeño peppers. Later, as my husband slept, my little daughter made very sure I understood she wasn't amused by jalapeño peppers, either.

No matter. As I drifted off to sleep, I thought of a name for her. And when she popped out four months later, she gave me a look that indicated that she wasn't amused by this little turn of events, either.

Ilsa J. Bick

I LOVE YOU MORE

Meet my daughter, Amanda. Four years old and a fountain of knowledge. The other day she was reciting a list of all the facts and tidbits shc has memorized. "One plus one is two. If you mix yellow paint with blue you get green. Penguins can't fly." . . . On and on she went.

Finally, she finished. "Mom," she said, looking very smug, "I know everything."

I acted as if I believed her, but chuckled to myself thinking of all the this-and-that's that a four-year-old child couldn't possibly know. Comparing her four years to my almost three decades of life experiences, I felt sure I knew what she knew and then some.

Within a week, I would learn I was wrong.

It all began as we were standing in front of the bathroom mirror, while I fixed Amanda's fine blonde hair. I was putting the final elastic on a spunky pair of ponytails and finished with, "I love you, Amanda."

"And, I love you," she replied.

"Oh, yeah," I taunted, "well I love you *more.*"

Her eyes lit up as she recognized the cue for the start of another "I love you more" match. "Nuh-uh," she laughed, "I love you the most."

"I love you bigger than a volcano!" I countered—a favorite family phrase in these battles of love.

"But, Mom, I love you from here to China." A country she's learning about thanks to our new neighbors up the street.

We volleyed a few favorite lines. "I love you more than peanut butter. . . . Well, I love you more than television. . . . I even love you more than bubble gum."

It was my turn again, and I made the move that usually brings victory. "Too bad, chickadee. I love you bigger than the universe!" On this day, however, Amanda was not going to give up. I could see she was thinking.

"Mom," she said in a quiet voice, "I love you more than myself."

I stopped. Dumbfounded. Overwhelmed by her sincerity.

Here I thought that I knew more than she did. I thought I knew at least everything that she knew. But I didn't know this.

My four-year-old daughter knows more about love than her twenty-eight-year-old mom. And somehow she loves me more than herself.

Christie A. Hansen

THE CAP

It was a darling cap. It was crocheted with angora yarn, and attached to the soft peak at the top was a little ball of angora fuzz. Strings tied the cap securely under the chin.

Our little girl was six years old when we purchased the cap, and because of her susceptibility to earaches, we made sure she never left the house in the winter without it. But she *hated* that cap! She would think of any "reason" in the world *not* to wear it. Once she exhausted all excuses, she simply hid it.

One morning when the school-bus driver honked for her, we were again searching for the cap! "But I didn't hide it last night," our daughter wailed pitifully.

"You've hidden it before, so why should I believe you?" I asked.

Exasperated, I hurried her out the door to the waiting bus. Calling after her, I shouted, "Don't cry to me tonight when you have an earache!"

I closed my door and the bus drove away. As I gathered the laundry, my anger built. She knew exactly where she had hidden the cap. Muttering, I opened the washing machine and there I saw The Cap! Just where I had thrown it the night before!

How ashamed I felt. I paced the floor watching the clock. It would be 9:15 before first recess. Could I wait that long to tell her how sorry I was?

At 9:00, I drove up to school and parked by the playground. Finally, the bell rang, and the first-graders streamed out for recess. There she was! I stepped outside the car and called to her. Her face lit up when she saw me and she bounced toward me.

"It's my mommy!" she squealed to the friends who followed her. She threw her little arms around me, genuinely glad to see me. As I hugged her to me, tears filled my eyes.

"Oh, Lucinda," I cried. "I am so sorry. I found your cap where I put it last night. Can you please forgive me?" She looked puzzled for a moment, hugged me and, giggling, ran quickly back to play.

Years later, I found papers and notes from her college classes. As I opened one of her old notebooks, I came across an assignment sheet that an English professor had given her. The instructions on it were to write a paper about an incident in your life that had profoundly affected you.

Stapled to the sheet was the essay she had written. It was entitled, simply, "The Cap." Across the top, the professor had written a glowing critique of the paper and marked it with an A-plus.

The final paragraph of the essay summed up the effect "the cap incident" had on her life: ". . . and I learned that I had a mother who could not only admit it when she made a mistake, but would even apologize for it. . . ."

Molly Lemmons

THE COMPETITION

Me, again?

The band director looked sympathetic when he came to me. "Lori, I am sorry to ask you again, especially since you spent so much time making these new flags for us, but I need someone to pick up the flags during finals competition tonight."

"Aw, Tom, I really wanted to see the new flags from the stands today. I worked the preliminary competition. Isn't there anyone else?"

Tom looked around and saw the backs of the other parents as they wound their way into the football stadium seats. "You know how it is, Lori. I'd really love to tell you I can find someone else, but I'll be honest. I've already asked several of the parents and they all said they couldn't do it. I know it's unfair for me to ask you, but. . . ."

I smiled at the distraught band director and patted my old friend's arm, "It's okay, I'll see them on the videotape. I'll do it."

He looked so relieved I had to laugh. "Now, go get your band ready, Mr. Stout. I'll see you later."

Knowing the routine well, I walked toward the pit crew to wait with them until we were told to take the field for competition. While I waited, I glared up into the stadium seats at the other parents as they greeted each other and took their seats. My eyes narrowed as I stared up at them and I certainly was enjoying the pity party I was throwing myself. *How dare they?* I thought. *Why do they think they never have to do the work and that I'm always so happy to do it?*

I felt a tug on my sleeve and glanced over to see one of the drummers hesitate beside me. "We've been told to take the field,

Mrs. Bottoms," he said quietly. "It's time to go."

Shaking myself out of my pity party, I patted the drummer on the back, whispered, "Let's get 'em!"

He smiled, the tension disappeared and I followed him onto the field with the band.

Out of the corner of my eye, I caught a glimpse of my daughter as she carried her armload of flags onto the field. Her colorguard uniform shone gold under the stadium lights as she set her flags in their waiting position, then turned and took her first flag with her to her starting position.

The announcer's voice boomed over the loudspeaker, "The Pride of Broken Arrow—you may take the field!"

The drum major's whistle sounded, and the band began to thrill the crowd. Together, as if all 200 kids were one unit, they swayed with military precision, first this way, then that, each student knowing exactly where he needed to be. Even from the sidelines, the perfect cadences amazed me. Their music was astounding and flawless.

I was shaken out of my revelry as the first song ended, and the color guard rushed to the front lines to drop their flags, crouched to pick up their rifles and waited for their cue. I knew what to do. I bent low and began to run from one end of the line to the other, picking up the discarded flags as I went. I lost track of where I was and concentrated on picking up each flag as I ran.

Suddenly, I was at the end of the line and I quietly laid the flags in a pile to be picked up as we left the field. A pause in the playing helped me hear the whisper. The little voice reached me and it sounded like, "I love you, Mom." It was then that I realized I was bending very near my daughter. I looked around, and my eyes locked with hers. Her smile told me it was her words that had reached me. She winked, heard her cue and moved back onto the field without missing a beat.

The rest of the evening went by quickly, and soon it was time for the awards ceremony. All ten finals bands marched proudly onto the field to await the competition's results. My work was done, so I started to fade away into the crowd, but as I was walking away, the band director caught my arm and said, "Come on, you are going onto the field with us."

I was surprised, but I understood he was trying to make up for my missing the show from the stands. Smiling, I followed the band and proudly stood with the directors at the back of the field.

We took our share of awards that night, but we still held our breath as the announcer boomed over the intercom, "And the winner for this competition is . . . The Pride of Broken Arrow!"

As the drum major accepted the award, the band was near to bursting with excitement. I could feel the electricity in the air while the kids stood at attention waiting for the director to dismiss them.

The announcer once more, "Congratulations to all of tonight's bands. This concludes the ceremonies."

Tom turned to his band and said, "Way to go, kids!"

Then he nodded at the drum major who said, "Band dismissed!"

Pandemonium. The kids screamed, they hugged, they jumped in the air. I spotted my daughter across the sea of band members and watched as she made her way toward me. She threw her arms around my neck and noisily kissed my cheek. We looked into each other's eyes and shared a precious moment that required no words.

As she spotted her friend and ran from my side, I looked up at the parents in the stadium stands. I watched them applauding with excitement and thought with a smile, *I don't think I'll tell them how much they've missed tonight.*

Lori A. Bottoms

MY CHILDREN

Sometimes I sit and wonder
where I would be today,
had I made different choices,
changed my path along the way.

Could I have mastered greatness,
had a lifetime full of bliss?
Which roads could I have taken,
and which ones did I miss?

But when I see your faces,
a reflection of my life,
all worldly goods diminish
under years of toil and strife.

For you my darling children,
are the masterpiece I'll leave.
The greatness that I longed for,
at last, I did, achieve.

Donna J. Calabro

HAPPY RETURNS

"Happy birthday, Jane!"

Inwardly, I groaned. Couldn't our too-efficient receptionist have forgotten to consult her calendar just this once?

"Thanks, Carol." I tried to inject enthusiasm into my tone as I zoomed into my office. The less said about this momentous occasion the better.

However, by leaning forward at her desk, Carol could look through the open doorway right at my desk. This she did, beaming a huge smile at me. "Lordy, lordy, look who's forty! Planning a big celebration tonight?"

"Nah. Just family."

My mother would probably bring over a cake, and my sole hope for the day was that it would be her Heavenly Chocolate, full of fruit and nuts and spices. Kathy had the night off from the movie theater where she worked part-time—"shoveling popcorn," as she put it—and Stewart would have finished his paper route long before I got home. We would sit down together to something quick and simple, maybe the tacos the kids liked. No romantic candlelit dinners for this birthday girl.

Carol's smile widened, if that was possible. "It's nice with just family."

Faker that I was, I agreed, then grabbed my coffee mug and scurried off. Unfortunately, to get to the kitchen, I had to pass through the art department. One of the designers looked up and chortled, "Over the hill now, huh, Jane?"

"Rub it in, Bill," I grumbled. Still on the sunny side of thirty, Bill just grinned.

Another designer, Dottie, was a little more perceptive, and with good reason. At about forty-five, she was even more shopworn than I was.

"You know what the French say, don't you?" She peered up at me slyly through her auburn bangs. "They don't think a woman is even worth noticing till she's forty."

I grimaced. "I don't know any Frenchmen."

She just gave me a throaty chuckle and went back to the ad she was comping. I filled my mug and skulked back to my office. My desk was turned so that my back was to the raw January day outside, but I seemed more than capable of making my own gloom.

Bill was right; I was over the hill. And I hadn't exactly reached much of a pinnacle on the way, either. As I slurped coffee, I summarized in my head: I had achieved no real career, just a low-paying job as a small-time copywriter. I had salted away no bank account. I had provided my children with none of the things they assured me all their friends had—VCR, microwave, answering machine, vacations. Worst of all for one who had spent her childhood playing Cinderella, I had failed—both in my marriage and during the three years since—to find true love.

Even so, the minutes were ticking away, as fast as they had for four decades, and the billing sheet in front of me was waiting for entries. So I applied myself to the task of writing a brochure for seed corn.

Seated as I was just five or six feet from the receptionist's desk, I had learned to tune out the opening of the front door, especially when I was under such enchantment as yield-per-acre. Therefore, I was a little startled when I heard an unfamiliar voice speak my name in a questioning tone.

I looked up. "Yes?" A man was standing in my doorway holding some sort of huge, shapeless mass covered in tissue paper.

"Flowers for you."

He stepped forward, deposited what he claimed to be flowers on the corner of my desk, and disappeared.

Carol took his place in the doorway and demanded, "Did somebody send you flowers?"

"I guess so," I replied, dazed.

"Some secret admirer you forgot to tell me about?"

I tried a shaky laugh. "I doubt that."

"Well, aren't you going to look at them?"

"Well . . . yeah." As I ripped away the tissue, I wondered if Carol could possibly be right. Had I somehow impressed one of the few men who had taken me out? My rational side butted in to say that wasn't likely. Maybe the people in the office had taken pity on me, or some kind client.

The bouquet that emerged from the tissue paper was an enormous sheaf of springtime color—irises, daisies, carnations—quite a contrast with the scene outside my window. I was stunned.

"Well, see who they're from," practical Carol ordered.

I fumbled for the card. The tiny envelope bore my name in the unfamiliar handwriting of someone at the florist shop. Then I pulled out the card itself.

"Dear Mom." I smiled as I recognized the self-conscious, curlicue letters I had watched develop for a dozen years. "Today, life begins, right? Love, Me."

My eyes stung. Of course. Who else could it have been but Kathy? Kathy, who had lent me her favorite top because she thought I had nothing suitable to wear to a party. Who had once found me sitting alone in the dark and whispered, "Mom, what's wrong?" Who had offered to split weekend nights out with me so someone would always be home with Stewart.

I reached out and started touching petals. Each festive pastel made a memory spring forth, and I thought with tender dismay that my hard-working daughter could ill afford such an extravagant gesture.

Dottie appeared next to Carol. “Oooh, flowers! Who from?”

I blinked against my tears and said proudly, “My daughter.”

“Aaaw,” Carol cooed. “That’s so sweet.”

I could tell it was more of an effort for Dottie. “That’s very nice.”

My only answer was the radiant smile a woman is supposed to wear on her birthday. I just couldn’t hide the fact that I had found true love.

Jane Robertson

FIRST KISS

I have been replaced as the main woman in my son's life.

At five, he has a girlfriend. Actually, two. It would have been three, but one ran him over with her tricycle and that was the end of their relationship.

It used to be I was the woman who was worshipped. My son looked to me to define cool. I picked out his clothes. I was the authority on how tall he would be someday if he ate all his vegetables. I decided how his hair was cut. I decorated his room. I was *the* woman.

But not anymore.

It all came to an end one day when my son, Junior, came home from preschool, brushed a hand across his brow and said, "I've had a hard day, Mom. Eva* was chasing me and kissing me all day long."

Excuse me?

I don't recall kissing in preschool. Actually, I don't recall preschool. But I do recall my first kiss with Benny Nunez behind the backstop in the first grade. So I told Junior that he couldn't kiss Eva, and that he should tell the teacher when Eva chased him.

But somehow I think my rule went unheeded. I mean, if a pretty girl chases you and kisses you, are you really going to tell the teacher?

No, not if you are Junior and whipped into shape by four-year-old Eva. She is very picky, little Eva. If Junior dares to wear an uncool Bob the Builder shirt, she won't be seen with him. He lets her have the good stuff from his lunch. And if I dare to remind him at dinner about vegetables and their associated growing properties, well, Eva can contradict me even if she isn't there.

I do not think I would be a good mother-in-law to Eva.

You see, I'm a little tired of Eva's demands. First, Junior's hair wasn't right. It was flat, not spiky. And it didn't have dyed tips. Junior begged for spiky, dyed tips just like another boy in school. A boy Eva thought was cool. Each day, I was told heartrending stories of how Eva liked the other boy better. And if Junior could just have dyed spikes in his hair, too, Eva would like him again.

I started to give in. I really did. I figured it didn't matter and I could cut the spikes off before kindergarten started in September.

But my husband was not one with that plan. And neither was my sister, our hairdresser. I was sure as heck not going to dye the tips of my wiggling five-year-old's hair. So we bought hair gel that is colored.

It didn't go over well with Eva.

Junior thought he was one cool dude, with yellow gunk in his hair, spiking it up perfectly. Junior's martial arts instructor thought it looked like a dinosaur egg had been cracked on Junior's head. I even thought Junior was nuts. It took two hair washings every night to get the yellow gunk out of his hair so it didn't stain his pillowcase.

Most important, Eva thought he was a geek, and the chasing and kissing stopped.

It looked like heartbreak for my boy, but the unthinkable happened. A new girl came to preschool. Eva got replaced.

Oh, the fickle heart of a pre-kindergartner.

At first, the new girl was only called "girlfriend." Junior has trouble remembering names, the same trouble his father has (his father also has trouble with dates, so I remind him of every birthday and anniversary well ahead of time). Anyway, after a few days of my prodding, Junior discovered that "girlfriend's" real name was Madison*.

Madison worshipped Junior, but didn't really want to change him the way Eva did. This was an incredibly good thing. She didn't care about how Junior looked. She didn't care if his clothes were cool or not. She didn't tell him that the Blue's Clues Applesauce Junior adores is only for babies. She didn't chase him and kiss him.

Madison would make a great daughter-in-law.

Unfortunately, Madison came along just as Junior's preschool experience ended. He's a big boy now, you know. He starts kindergarten in September and his two younger women won't be there.

I'm sure we'll start the same cycle over again. I camn only hope that Junior learns to run faster and that his next crush likes him the way he is—flat hair, uncool school uniform and all.

**Names have been changed to protect my future daughters-in-law.*

Laurie A. Sontag

MAPLE LEAF WARS

I watched him scamper outside, a bed of gold and red leaves beckoning him. *Come play with us, little man!*

He raced as fast as his little legs could carry him, and with a "wheeeee," threw himself into the arms of his autumn friends. They played with him, covered him, snuck down his jacket, tripped him and tickled him. My carefully piled leaves soon became a playhouse, a castle, a battleground, a space ship.

"Come play, Momma!"

I smiled at him from the kitchen window and shook my head. It was an encouraging smile, but there was no way Momma was going to get out of her fuzzy slippers and oversized tee to go out there. C-c-c-cold . . .

Lost sight of him now . . . buried under there. *Oh dear is he warm enough?* I ran through a mental checklist and nodded yep.

"Woooooossssssshhhhhhhhh!!" My trouper surfaced.

"Captain to starship, we got the leaf leader, need backup!"

"He's gonna havta tell us where the others are hiding! Send Poliwhirl and Pikachu with double stun phasers!"

He spun around hit by a falling leaf, staggered, clutched his Star Wars tuque and keeled over.

"Aaargh . . . he got me, stoopid poxamity radar dint work."

"I'm wounded, gotta . . . get . . . to . . . ship."

He crawled forward to the tree trunk, his little mitted hands reached for the root of the tree that was his teleporter.

"Drop it, Human!"

He gasped and looked up.

There was Queen Momma Leaf, in full battle regalia with King Daddy's coat, scarf thrown decadently around my neck, ten starleaves stuck in my tuque signifying my position as Her Royal Autumness.

"We have you surrounded, Human, prepare to be tickled!"

I dove at him, wrestling him, aided by my trusty leaf regiment.

Hmm . . . not that cold out here after all.

High-pitched squeals filled the air as the leaf queen did battle with the miniature human. Momma-toned shouts echoed as we rolled and pummeled each other into submission. A chance glance at the home ship window revealed King Daddy looking through, concerned but half amused, considering his options of committing the queen on account of insanity. Other spaceship windows showed neighbors shaking their heads or nodding with smiles, depending on the amount of bran in their diets. This momentary distraction cost me dearly as, with a victory yell, the Captain grabbed my queenly tuque and raced off with it.

"I got the old bag's hat!" he yelled into his transponder.

Note to self: Be careful when discussing Aunt Gladys in front of the captain.

The now tuqueless queen recovers quickly since no hat meant disheveled hair festooned with leaves would ruin my reputation in the galaxy for coiffure perfection.

I race after the short but cute Captain.

"Give it back you tinytwoleggedtestosteronetesttube! Queen Leaf demands it in the name of all things falling south!"

He stared at me.

"Huh?"

"Never mind son."

I made a flying tackle, taking advantage of his temporary bemusement at his archenemy's obvious Alzheimer's.

"Argggggh!!"

Falling prey to the universal mistake all Queen Autumnesses make after they've passed thirty by several light years, and still think they can accomplish flying tackles without squishing their boobs and causing trauma to bones carefully wrapped in cellulite spacesuits, I managed to squish my boobs and hurt my cellulite-wrapped spacesuit.

"Mom? Are you okay?" asked the now-concerned Captain.

"Uhmm . . . yes, I'm fine."

Pride has a way of relieving most moments of destruction, especially since Spaceship 212 across the street had that nosy three-headed alien with her nose stuck to her window watching me.

I chased the Captain around the trees and into the leaf settlements until he tired.

"Momma? Can you and me do this every day?"

"No, baby, but I'm sure Daddy and you can."

I smiled at the Captain as I collected him in my arms and strolled back to home base.

Nope . . . not cold out here at all.

Nathalie K. Taghaboni

A MOTHER'S LOVE

At one time children made May Day baskets to celebrate spring and the rewards of anonymous giving. When I was in perhaps the third grade, our class embarked on such an adventure. For several days, we worked on creating paper baskets. We cut colorful strips of construction paper and wove them together, following a magic formula shared by our teacher, Miss Anderson. We cut and wove and glued. Then we decorated them with our crayons and more cutting and gluing. Finally, we stapled handles onto the tops so that we could hang our creations on the doors of unsuspecting recipients: surely our mothers.

We were finished right on time. Miss Anderson brought armloads of flowers for us to use in stuffing our prizes. Lilacs and tulips and all the colorful flowers of spring. We had to wait until the day was nearly over before we were allowed to choose the flowers that were just right for our baskets. I chose the biggest, most beautiful blossoms, allowing myself to be selfish for the sake of my mother. Then we fidgeted away what remained of our day, waiting for the clock to tick down the minutes to our release.

Finally, mercifully, the bell rang! We threw on our coats, gathered our homework and our lunch pails, tied on our scarves and then, carefully, we cradled our offerings of love and off we ran to our individual homes!

I was so excited! I ran as fast as I could down the hill, across the street, up the block, heading home. I paused at the corner of my house, behind the hydrangea, to catch my breath and savor the moment. Then I glanced down to admire my offering one last time before I hung it lovingly over the doorknob. Horrors!! Shock, dread and dismay! My flowers were gone!

Apparently, bouncing out on my mad dash home, all that was left was a sad, smudged-up, wrinkled little paper-simulation of a basket. An empty vessel! I stood on the porch and burst into mournful sobbing tears.

By and by, my mom came to the door to discover the source of the anguish. As she let me in and helped me off with my coat and relieved me of my school things, I tried to relate my horrible dilemma. Through spasmodic agonies of hot teary mutterings, I tried to communicate the depth of my sorrow. As she listened, she wiped my brow with a cool damp cloth and stroked my hair with the other. Finally spent, I collapsed into her arms. Next, she did what I will never forget. She retrieved a paring knife from the kitchen and my poor little empty basket from the coffee table, and we went outside. Along the west side of the house there was a flowerbed. Many of our flowers had already bloomed. And, for more varieties, it was too soon for their showy displays. But we had blue bells! A whole big row of blue bells! She cut one and placed it in my basket. Then, she looked at me and handed me the knife (yes, she entrusted me with a SHARP KNIFE!) Then she retreated to the house to start dinner.

Slowly, as I cut the flowers and arranged them in my little paper basket, my enthusiasm began to return. I became intrigued with the little blue bells. Instead of a kaleidoscope of competing colors, my basket was in harmony with itself and nature. All a serene shade of blue. And, simultaneously, I was becoming serene. Cut and arrange, cut and arrange. Soon, once again, my gift was ready to be offered.

Now, a new emotion came over me. It dawned on me that the element of surprise, so essential to my deed, was now totally gone. Awkwardly, I placed the paper handle over the knob, knocked hesitantly, and made an embarrassed retreat. Mother slowly came and answered the door. Oh! She was SO surprised!

Could it be that she had forgotten? Yes! She had totally forgotten! The May Day surprise worked! She had no idea, no idea whatsoever, who had left the lovely gift! I stepped out of my hiding place. "Well, Mary Kay!" she exclaimed! "Look what someone left on our porch! Aren't they lovely!" With her excitement all my trepidations vanished. I fairly danced across the yard and into her arms. We went into the house and found our loveliest vase, a fruit jar, and placed the surprise gift of love into fresh water to display on the kitchen table. My pride of giving barely allowed me to maintain my anonymity. Mother was so thrilled to have been remembered on May Day that she didn't even ponder the identity of her benefactor.

That was around forty-five years ago. The blue bells and little woven basket are long gone. But the love endures.

Mary K. Schram

WISHING AWAY

Do you believe that some people are sent into your life to teach you an important lesson? I do! One such special person in my life was Katherine.

At the time I met Katherine, I was an extremely busy single mother, raising three rambunctious children. Life seemed to be a continual merry-go-round of work, home, schedules and activities. My fondest wish involved a deserted island with warm sunny days, an inexhaustible supply of romance novels, and quiet peace.

I became aware that Katherine had moved into my apartment complex when my seven-year-old daughter, Amber, asked if her new friend could spend the night. "Please? Her name is Joy, and she just moved into number 18 with her mommy."

I stopped making hamburger patties long enough to gaze at my child. Standing next to her was a blue-eyed, blonde-haired, gap-toothed little girl, waiting anxiously for my response. Issuing a resigned sigh, I agreed. "Go get Joy's things. We'll be eating in a half-hour." With big grins, the two pint-sized whirlwinds were gone. I continued dinner preparations, wishing that I could be ordering steak in a fine restaurant.

Within minutes, the phone rang. Katherine was calling to introduce herself and to confirm the invitation to spend the night. As we chatted, I noted that her words slurred occasionally, and wondered if she had a speech impediment. I had little time to ponder Katherine's speech, however. I had children to feed, laundry to do, and evening rituals to perform. With a hurried good-bye, I began peeling potatoes as I wished for the late-evening hours when I could retreat to my personal oasis called "my time."

From that beginning, Joy and Amber were inseparable. I spoke to Katherine on the phone occasionally, but never found the time to meet her. I would glimpse her sitting on a bench by the apartment playground, talking to the children, and wonder how she managed to find the time to spend on such frivolous activity. Didn't she have a job to go to? Housework to do? Schedules to keep? How I wished I knew the secret of finding time to play. What fun it would be to toss a ball and laugh in the summer sun.

As time passed, I began to notice that Katherine had problems. At times her speech was difficult to understand. She seemed to stagger and lose her balance. She dropped things. I wondered if she had an alcohol problem, and if the girls were safe with her. I decided the time had come to get to know this woman better, and invited her to a family dinner.

The evening that Katherine and Joy came to dinner proved to be a pivotal point in my life. I watched her closely as she sat at the table surrounded by children. Her speech was muffled in spots;

her movements measured and slow. But, I could not detect alcohol on her breath, and she declined the glass of wine I offered.

She seemed happy to focus on the children, listening intently to their stories. She asked them questions and considered their answers seriously. She flittered from topic to topic, keeping pace with their rapid thoughts. She entertained them with amusing stories of her own childhood.

After our meal, the children raced outside to play in what was left of the summer sunshine. Katherine and I followed at a more sedate pace. She walked slowly and carefully while she revealed her past life as a budding executive married to an active, high profile man. She told me of a lifestyle filled with social activity, vacations, and diverse people and settings. She had lived the life I'd always wished for and never achieved.

We settled on a bench beside the playground, and quietly watched the children at their games. I thought of how predictable and unexciting my life was compared to the picture Katherine had painted. With a sigh I told her how I wished the children were older. Then I would have more time to do some things for myself.

A small smile crossed her face as Katherine replied, "My only wish is to be able to stay out of a nursing home until Joy is grown. You see, I have multiple sclerosis. It's slowly taking over my body. It's changed my entire life. My husband couldn't deal with being married to an invalid, and I couldn't keep up with my career. Now, all I want is to be able to raise my daughter. I want to share as much of her world as I can for as long as I can. I've learned to treasure every minute of every day with her, because I don't know how many more of those there are left."

Katherine turned to me, and with another smile, she continued, "Don't spend your life wishing away what you have. You never know when it will be gone."

Approaching darkness ended our conversation, as we became involved with herding our children to their baths and beds. But later that evening, in that quiet time between wakefulness and sleep, her words floated through my head and heart, as I resolved to appreciate my world, instead of wishing for something different.

Time passed quickly, as it always does. Joy and Amber progressed through childhood and adolescence. I spent as much time as I could with them and Katherine. Life was a kaleidoscope of excitement and joy, pain and sorrow. For each stage of development the girls experienced, it seemed Katherine's body claimed a price as she slowly deteriorated physically and mentally.

Katherine's wish was granted: She was able to watch Joy receive her high school diploma, go on to further her education and start a rewarding career.

Some of my many wishes were also granted. The children are

now raised and on their own, and I have time to pursue my interests. I have precious grandchildren to keep me focused on the wonders of the world, and friends and family to love and enjoy. And I carry with me the knowledge that I was granted something for which I never wished . . . the rewards of knowing Katherine and learning from her wisdom.

Lana Brookman

THE THINGS YOU NEVER DID

Looking back across the years
To when I was a kid,
I find myself remembering
All the things you never did.

You never made me feel unloved
When I did something wrong,
You just helped me learn my lesson,
And you never stayed angry long.

You never went back on a promise,
You were never too tired to play,
No matter what else there was to be done
In the course of your busy day.

You never forgot to kiss me good night
As you tucked me snug in my bed,
You never rushed out in a hurry,
Without a story being read.

You never said no when I asked for a ride
To a practice, a friend's or the mall,
You never missed one softball game,
Even though I never once hit the ball!

You never acted like I was a failure
When I didn't do well on a test,
With your encouragement I came to learn
The importance of doing my best.

You never skimped on giving advice,
(Whether I listened or not!)
I swore I would never admit it,
But your words always helped a lot.

You never made fun of my trendy clothes
Or the makeup I put on all wrong,
You were there to wipe away countless tears
When I felt like I'd never belong.

You never turned one of my friends away,
Or for that matter, ten,
You never complained when the music got loud
Or they all spent the night in our den.

You never made fun of my boyfriends
Or made light of my tales of woe,
And if you felt relieved at each break-up,
You never once let it show.

Now that I'm a mother too,
I finally understand
How hard it can be to say the right thing
Or reach out with a tender hand.

I haven't said this near enough,
But Mom, I hope you know—
That all those things you never did
Are why I love you so.

Lisa Inquagiato Benwitz

I CAN'T REMEMBER

My pregnant friend complains of a backache and tired feet.
"Was it like this for you?" she asks.
I bury my face in your newborn hair
And I answer, "I can't remember."

I hear a new mother talking of her sleepless nights.
"Does everyone go through this?" she wearily says.
I watch you tottering on your fat little feet
And think to myself, I can't remember.

"When will he learn to eat on his own or tell me his needs?"
A frustrated mother laments.
I look into your three year old eyes, gleaming with independence.
When it got there? I can't remember.

"These two-year-old tantrums are driving us mad!
How did you cope?" an exasperated couple inquires.
I watch as you happily skip off to school
And I murmur, "I can't remember."

"My teenager rebels at everything! He won't even keep his room clean!
What did you do with your adolescent?" a burdened parent entreats.
I look around at your unused room, everything in place
And sigh, "I can't remember."

You hand me my newborn grandchild and with a beaming face you
announce,
"Oh, Mom, he's so wonderful! Did you ever feel this way?"
I hold him close and with tears in my eyes
I breathe, "Oh, how I remember!"

Barbara Nicks

THREE SQUEEZES

I drive while trying to keep myself detached from the woman in the passenger seat. She is my mother and she is mumbling about people doing "this, that and the other," as she puts it. None of what she's saying is positive. She is having a cranky day.

Good, I think. *That makes it easier.*

I'm taking her to her daycare center, the place she hates more than any other on Earth. It is a daycare center for people with Alzheimer's disease.

To make the painful drive easier, I perform what has become my driving ritual. I begin to imagine a brick wall going up between us. She talks her nonwords, strings of them, not making any sense at all, and I add brick after brick in my mind. I want the wall tight and secure. If it becomes weak, I start to remember her the way she used to be, the way she should be. And then I can't do what I need to do. How could I take her someplace she doesn't want to go? So I try to forget who she is, much as she has forgotten me, by adding the bricks and driving on in silence.

But then she does something that crumbles the wall. She reaches over and grabs my hand. Before I can pull away, she squeezes it three times. One, two, three . . . and the wall comes down.

Ever since I can remember, my mom and I have had our secret squeeze. One squeeze for each word: I love you. She squeezed to give me courage on the first day of school. She squeezed to give me reassurance when I was a teenager and didn't want to hear her words. She squeezed to tell me she was sorry when we'd had an argument. She squeezed to say, "That's the one," as we looked at the white wedding gown in the window. And she squeezed when words stuck in her throat as I handed her a baby girl named Ellen. I love you. Silently. Just between us.

The wall torn down, I turn to face her. She says to me, "You're such a pretty girl, do you know that?"

The words are hard for her. Sometimes they come out wrong or go places she didn't intend.

"I'm not sure who you are," she says.

I tell her that I am her daughter. She looks surprised. I tell her that the baby in the back is her grandson.

This is the one act I don't mind performing in the drama of Alzheimer's. Every time I tell her that she has grandchildren, her eyes light up with tears and sometimes she squeals like a little girl in utter delight. She looks at him, as if for the first time, and he waves his two-year-old hand at her, used to the routine, used to the woman-child who is his grandmother.

"Oh, I wanted one of those!" she says. "I wanted one of those!"

I tell her that she had babies. I tell her that I am her baby, and she is my mother. She looks confused. She says my name, and I'm relieved she's remembered it. But she is confused as to who I am, nonetheless.

"I used to be your baby," I tell her. She laughs because this is funny to her.

"I don't know, I just don't know," she says. "But I have loved you forever." And then three more squeezes.

My tears come freely now. This causes her concern. Her brow furrowed, she rubs my hand.

"What's the matter? What can I do?" she says.

She sounds just like herself. Hopefully, I turn to face her, but with one quick glance I can see she's not there. She begins talking nonsense, about "those people" and all that they do wrong.

The magic settles and I start to rebuild the wall. I stop, however, after a couple of bricks. Instead I reach over and grab her hand. I squeeze it three times. She smiles at me and says again, "You're such a pretty girl. I have loved you forever."

She is sincere. She could pick me out of a crowd of thousands. She wouldn't know who I am, or be able to connect me with the baby that floats in and out of her memories, but she would know that she's loved me forever.

Three squeezes. Her way of telling me that all is not lost. Her way of telling me her heart has not forgotten. Her way of telling me, of all the things she did in her life, I was the most important.

Carol Tokar Pavliska

HANDS OF TIME

Those graceful and elegant fingers braided my hair, made my lunches, and brushed away my tears. Frightened animals stopped quivering when she laid her hands upon them. Those hands prepared our dinner, set the table, and then scoured away the remnants left behind. They rolled pie crust so delicate it would melt upon the tongue, and scrubbed stains from our clothes with a vengeance. The iron pump handle wielded to her will, spilling cool water into the bucket that hung from the spout.

Her nails were carefully tended by a monthly soaking in warm soapy water followed by a firm scrubbing with a small brush. An orange stick pushed the cuticles back, and a file shaped their ovals to perfection. Occasionally, a coat of clear polish completed the ritual.

Fancy scented creams were not an option—only the sensible healing ointments delivered by the Watkins man.

Throughout the years, I observed those beautiful hands as they ministered to the needs of our family. As time passed, her fingers picked up needle and thread, refusing to be idle. Under her touch, perfectly formed stitches matured into a plethora of colorful flowers, birds and full-skirted ladies adorning pillowcases that cradled our heads at night. Her hand-stitched quilts grace the bedrooms of children, grandchildren and great-grandchildren. Their beauty warms the soul as their weight warms the body.

Friends have told friends. From far and near, the requests come for her hand-stitched wonders. Every stitch done by hand, whether creating a small pillow or a bountiful covering for a king-size bed. Each creation is unique, a one-of-a-kind treasure.

Arthritis has tried to stake a claim, but her fingers defy it, refusing to give way to defeat. The freckles on the backs of her hands slowly turned into "age" spots, screaming that it was time to slow down. The once-smooth skin has become thinner, the veins playing peek-a-boo. But still her hands move, continuing to weave beauty with each newborn day.

My hands learned to braid hair, make lunches and brush away tears. I held my hand out to feel the down of a bird, the sleek fur of a cat, the deep coat of a dog. With patience, I would hold out my hand until they would approach. Their quivering would stop when I placed my hands upon them.

My hands can set an elegant table for company and scour the burned pans from my culinary attempts. I learned to roll pie crust. I once scrubbed our laundry, before the modern convenience of an automatic washer became available.

Though once I fought to draw water from the pump, today I turn a faucet and it appears, already warm or cold, depending on my choice.

My hands pinned cloth diapers on babies and today peel off the tape to secure a disposable diaper on my grandchildren. My fingers grace the keyboard of a computer, weaving words, as my mother weaved her needle and thread.

Gathering my thoughts, I look upon my hands tonight and behold the spectacle. My mother's hands have transposed themselves to my own body. The fingers are still graceful, feeling from time to time the twinge of arthritis, but refusing to slow down. A plastic pump bottle of hand lotion sits at my fingertips to be used at my leisure. Still, the "age" spots have appeared, and I see the veins playing peek-a-boo. I'm not sure when it happened, but the metamorphosis is complete.

My only prayer is that the hands that belonged to me have left behind memories that will be recalled with pleasure when my daughters notice their hands have evolved into mine.

Carol Ann Erhardt

CONTRIBUTORS

Lisa Inquagiato Benwitz began writing again after a hiatus of twenty years, when her husband and son taught her that it's never too late to dust off your dreams. In addition to writing rhyming poetry, personal essays and fiction, she and her parents run a freelance court reporting firm.

Ilsa J. Bick, M.D., is a child and adolescent, and forensic psychiatrist. She has published prize-winning short fiction in anthologies such as *Star Trek: Strange New Worlds* and *Writers of the Future*; and her work has appeared in *SCIFI.COM* and *Beyond the Last Star*, among many others. Her novel, Well of Souls, is forthcoming in November from Pocket Books.

Lori A. Bottoms enrolled at the local community college, when her oldest child left for college,. After graduating with a journalism degree, Lori worked as associate editor for local magazines. As she gained experience, she was able to begin working out of her home-office as a freelance writer and today her regular contributions can be found in magazines nationwide. While she is currently accepting new writing assignments, Lori is also working to get her first novel, *In an Instant,* through the publishing phase. She resides in Broken Arrow, Oklahoma in a partially empty nest—only husband Larry, two of her four children and dachshunds Hairy Bottoms and Seemore Bottoms remain in the home today. She can be reached at *WriterLoriWalker@aol.com.*

Lana Brookman, a Wisconsinite, teaches writing and speech for a technical college, and is a freelance writer. She enjoys reading, writing, music, playing on her computer and meeting people. Her goals include continuing to write, and visiting the nooks and crannies of the world. She can be reached at *purple@tomah.com.*

Donna J. Calabro resides in Indiana with her husband, Jim, and their children, Jimmy, Vincent and Katharine. She is a member of St. Patrick's Catholic Church and is a registered nurse. She can be reached at *djcalabro@yahoo.com.*

Carol Ann Erhardt lives in Columbus, Ohio with her husband Ron and their cat, Sarah. The things she enjoys most are reading, writing and tent camping. She is currently writing a romantic suspense novel, *Hit and Run.* You can read the first chapters at her Web site *www.novellady.com* or contact her at *carolann@novellady.com.*

Christie A. Hansen is the mother of three young children. From 1997 until 2000. she wrote a weekly self-syndicated parenting column, *From the Trenches.* A past column, "I'm Not Your Slave" also appears in the book, *Chicken Soup for the Parent's Soul.* She can be reached at *hansenchristie@yahoo.com.*

Molly Lemmons has worked for the Mustang, Oklahoma Public Schools for the past twenty-one years. She enjoys swimming, writing, and her seven cats. Her book, *Kind of Heart,* short stories about life in the 1950s, went on sale in 2000. She can be reached at *mollyloubelle @cox.net* or sign in on her Web site at *www.homestead.com/mollylou/mollylou.html.*

Barbara Nicks taught school in Portugal, traveled throughout Europe and did mission work on the Amazon until she discovered her greatest mission—being a wife and the mother of two boys. She has also been an elementary-school teacher in Texas for fifteen years. She can be reached at *bnicks@email.com.*

Jane Robertson is a staff editor for the nature magazine, *Snowy Egret,* and reviews movies online for *crosshome.com.* She contributed to the Dawkins Project's upcoming *CELEBRATIONS: Notes to My Grandfather* and to Kimberly Ripley's next *Breathe Deeply* collection. She can be reached at *janerobe@yahoo.com.*

Mary K. Schram lives in Puyallup, Washington with her husband, David. She has two sons and a daughter. Mary enjoys cooking and gardening and quilting and is a lover of words and dark chocolate and small town America. She is a numeric control programmer for a large aerospace firm.

Laurie A. Sontag is a California writer and mother who wishes parenthood had come with a how-to guide. Her column appears weekly in the *Gilroy Dispatch.* Her award-winning work can also be seen at *Sanitycentral.com* and is available for distribution via the Humor News Service. She can be reached at *www.lauriesontag.com.*

Nathalie K. Taghaboni is a freelance writer in Caribbean dialect and standard English. She also directs the North American operations of *SHE Caribbean* magazine. Nathalie enjoys biking, music and tutors grades one through four at her son's elementary school. Nathalie host a humor Web site called Commess University. She can be reached at *nathalie@taghaboni.com.*

Permissions

The Day It All Came Together. Reprinted by permission of Ilsa J. Bick, M.D. ©2002 Ilsa J. Bick, M.D.

I Love You More. . . . Reprinted by permission of Christie Austin Hansen. ©2000 Christie Austin Hansen.

The Cap. Reprinted by permission of Molly Lemmons. ©2002 Molly Lemmons. From KIND OF HEART ©Quality Publications.

The Competition. Reprinted by permission of Lori A. Bottoms. ©2002 Lori A. Bottoms.

My Children. Reprinted by permission of Donna J. Calabro. ©2002 Donna J. Calabro.

Happy Returns. Reprinted by permission of Jane Robertson. ©2002 Jane Robertson.

First Kiss. Reprinted by permission of Laurie A. Sontag. ©2001 Laurie A. Sontag.

Maple Leaf Wars. Reprinted by permission of Nathalie K. Taghaboni. ©1999 Nathalie K. Taghaboni.

A Mother's Love. Reprinted by permission of Mary K. Schram. ©2003 Mary K. Schram.

Wishing Away. Reprinted by permission of Lana Brookman. ©2000 Lana Brookman.

The Things You Never Did. Reprinted by permission of Lisa Inquagiato Benwitz. ©2001 Lisa Inquagiato Benwitz .

I Can't Remember. Reprinted by permission of Barbara Nicks. ©1997 Barbara Nicks.

Three Squeezes. Reprinted by permission of Carol T. Pavliska. ©2001 Carol T. Pavliska.

Hands of Time. Reprinted by permission of Carol Ann Erhardt. ©2002 Carol Ann Erhardt.